MY PLANET OF KITES

OTHER BOOKS BY THE AUTHOR

Je Te Trouve Belle Mon Homme (Écrits des Forges, 2012)

Le Windex de Narcisse (Michel Brûlé Éditeur, 2007)

MY PLANET OF KITES

MARIE-ÈVE COMTOIS

Translated from the French
by Stuart Ross & Michelle Winters

Mansfield Press

Library and Archives Canada Cataloguing in Publication

Comtois, Marie-Ève, 1980-
[Je te trouve belle mon homme. English]
My planet of kites / Marie-Ève Comtois ; translated by Stuart Ross and Michele Winters.

Poems.
Translation of: Je te trouve belle mon homme.
ISBN 978-1-77126-061-9 (pbk.)

I. Ross, Stuart, translator II. Winters, Michele, translator III. Title. IV. Title: Je te trouve belle mon homme. English.

PS8605.O548J413 2014 C841'.6 C2014-905717-2

Editor for the press: Stuart Ross
Typesetting: Stuart Ross

The publication of *My Planet of Kites* has been generously supported by the Canada Council for the Arts and the Ontario Arts Council.

ONTARIO ARTS COUNCIL
CONSEIL DES ARTS DE L'ONTARIO
an Ontario government agency
un organisme du gouvernement de l'Ontario

Canada Council for the Arts
Conseil des arts du Canada

Mansfield Press
25 Mansfield Avenue, Toronto, Ontario, Canada M6J 2A9
Publisher: Denis De Klerck
www.mansfieldpress.net

I'm still a tenant. Voyage, voyage *desireless*, I feel like a voyage myself. I have leukemia without my suitcase. I could have a pal, my pal is me. We like the same music, set sail without supplies. My grandmother never taught me to play piano, but I heard her sing and play. Your life outruns your age, you look like a little boy in your Metallica sweater.

Alexandre, what are we in this city, a new set of books, What Do I Know? We were still up when daylight streamed through the window and we were frightened, as though we could walk out of an asylum. I'm deep in my darkness, pursued by zebras. Joan Baez bores me, but I'm so sharp and excited. The feast of our illusions sustains us throughout the day. Ah, life, life. pasfaciledenerienfaire.com

I'd like to buy, in a tube from DeSerres, the blue of this night, the twelfth of July, 2009. Pour me a glass of hot country, Montreal is freezing. We are not famous, because we adore the rain. I am also as sad as a team of one. Let us be eloquent and filled with radiant insects. I love you at the end of the day.

What are you up to tomorrow? I'm taking time off to write about the unreal boredom of taking time off. I'm living my life like a novel that no one reads. I'm not bragging about writing a twenty-page novel. I know that living disarms me, fill my shoes with little soldiers. I am a ghost weary of identity.

You told me to stay calm, I waited in my chair. You drink wine with the gay and the famous, you take off with the whiskey at the end of the night, you gulp down the last of the stars. It's *truly* dark when you've had some whiskey.

The forest's evaporation triggers insomnia among the butterflies. I put my orange chair on the balcony, and put myself in the chair. Dance a rigadoon in your cotton clothes, tomorrow it will be fine. I would paint a rainfall, but it always turns out like fireworks. Beneath the November Rain, umbrellas look like suns. We're francophone like xylophones.

I'm mixed up about how I present myself, in a month we'll no longer recognize each other. With ice, water is absolutely delicious. On the weekend, we discuss astrology and we're tired because the phone rings at midnight while we're sound asleep. In 2004, I had a neighbour who listened to Guns N' Roses. I pass by hints of so many women.

Am I autonomous? Rejecting any kind of dependence. Dancing at the edge of the lake like a kayak indistinguishable from the waves. To stay quiet amid the passion. Be silent, read books and check out films. Slow down, without your beige coat you'll freeze in the elevator. Don't forget to hurl flowers out the car window. You don't have a car.

I was thinking about going for a bike ride when this *guy* said to me, “Hi, how’s it going?” and I unplugged the answering machine. I’ll watch hockey alone this winter with my glass of milk. Hope arises when I cover the paper with blue lines. Bernard, you are hacking even the personalities of the computers, you almost never laughed. I’m not sure I’ll survive the works of Cioran. Fire is destroying the apartments on Plateau-Mont-Royal.

I'm not a poet, I've got a permanent ache deep in my heart. Wasting time on Facebook is like an eraser shaped like a pencil. If only I could feel really beautiful, curious and devoted. A woman among women. It's possible to succeed. Take me in your arms, comb my hair, unbuckle my sandals. You cure my desire for the psychiatric, why have you gone?

C'est une belle journée, *Punch-Drunk Love*. Don't leave, I'm full of advice. Dad. Mayan calendar. White as a sheet that you fold, close the eyes of the dead. We must suffer for our mothers' handicap rude gestures. Here here I am here with my lawless hammock.

Capricorne va changer le monde. I didn't wash my hair this morning before going to work. I'll go for a stroll on the moon. Drink one litre of water every day. Simone de Beauvoir stayed home on Mondays. They say that, we lie to ourselves.

You're telling your life story to everyone, just as well not to the friend of the wind, no one would lend you a coat. You don't even sleep in an idle bed, force wings on the heavens so it flies away, for you gaze as far as the laces in your laceless sandals. Go to heaven for good. Stop your sweets on the phone. You need to go, down some more pills.

Solange is dead and the plant is still talking. I can sleep with the help of meds and testify to my tired but functional life. Living on sixty dollars every two weeks—I can do that. Just next to the depressed, this tree barely worthy of trees depresses me, blech. You see the ashregas in the Carmelites, the pink flowers next to the marsetilla?

The bike in the heart of a child or the time to gently touch, stutters words words. Dalida lives out of happiness and love. She always sticks her nose in others' business. To play outside of my impressions of sunlit hens, I sleep in an insectarium while the insects wander. The turtle lake exists in the light-filled void, when a mountain dreams of the tip of the clouds, the deer come out.

Each truth flees from me, each time you fall on the floor covered in a thousand crows you don't belong to. I pray for the fame of our beautiful bodies. The truth tells you what to say, it's in my head. Hide in my ears so I can hear nothing but the patter of your ideas.

Soon I will live my thirty years in an armed celebration. Everyone wants to take me to the water. I can become a heron and switch lakes and plants to hide myself before I switch fears. My mother always watched me, I hid behind the cereal boxes.

Behind the photo of Mother Teresa was a glaring spelling mistake. The mistake concerned the word "realm." Nicole was already so deeply in the realm of exhaustion she ignored my observation. We work alongside our own performance.*

* Tough to find your place, the acceptable use of work time to pay rent and/or the patience it takes to read Michel Butor.

Stay at my place behind the couch, listening to songs on the computer. Main thing is, don't go to Emergency, stay away from hospitals. They lock you up in the psychiatrists' silence, look for your mother-scars. The gift of the Christmas-tree ambience is already here for next year. You've got an artist problem on your island. Put stains in your movie.

I turned the pages slowly, like a car hemmed in by other cars and unable to leave the parking lot. An ad caught my eye: “Sweaters—2 for the price of.” No one really knows what I’m talking about. My dinner looks like a cafeteria tray. The snow comes back to life for a moment in your beautiful house for a married couple.

In a snowball for amateur travellers, we're put off by white because it evokes the task of preserving the impossible. The cellphone sits motionless next to the straightening iron and the dead pens in a Liberté yogurt container. Even so, we throw out just about everything.

I wish for a life free of a *clean* obsession. Need sunlight in my lite life. From sugar to sand, an angel's filth I hold in my mittens to avenge the summer rain play Nintendo. I love you so much I hate you. The cleanliness of the soul purifies failed love.

My planet of kites, I think you're rather pretty. Your green jacket and your pink sweater, essential dove. Paix, Blue Velvet, lipstick fence. I live in an extraordinary world. Un monde ordinaire. Paradis. Blues NirVanana, Friday's grapefruit, bloody Cleopatra, Asterix murdered, Obelix travesty. Butterflies dance in the trees.

Let's glue eyes on eyelids, in wrong, in truth, in fiction, in the car. APPLE: the skin of soft eyes deserving of hope. We pass the time singing that story of the hairstylist daring the man to move away.

The urge to decorate an apartment with trees. Going to Timbuktu to catch a western show. Drinking sporty whale beer to hold on to the expectation of future death throes. Placing a ladder in the sea so the boats return to dry out in the shade of sunken jewels.

Fish eat soft food. I approve of the wind's pleasant violence in the tranquil stomachs of wolves. Breathe the right way, like the trees and the beauty of Montreal. I, I, I prefer McDonald's, you love Burger King. I was making supper to make you hungry.

Me, I don't really have a life, I'm affected by indifference the way others complain about lousy weather and think of their supper the way the table thinks of it. You have to leave a few dishes on the counter to feel like you exist in your apartment. Sometimes I feel good—in the corner of a restaurant, for example. My cat has short paws and I have a long life. I exist, I exaggerate.

In my Slovakian mood, I am wild before the horror as well as a bitten forehead, joyful dead sky. The tulip sings beneath the trees and the moon dances obliquely. Weep April's silence, weep a deep drowsiness, weep my heart. The fireworks resemble each Saturday night, perhaps those Saturdays resemble each other as well. Fire fire lovely lovely, bonjour Madame Sagan.

Tell me this blue that burns in the night, why did I buy it the 12th of July? We dread our faces of poems as red as the hair of Benoît, poet and musician of the streets of Quebec. I want a kind world, my friendliness is a feigned detention.

Polaroid season in the outdoor recreation centre in the Laurentians or out on a street corner. Camus' plague, clothes abandoned in a park, sad poem for Anne-Marie. You seem more womanly with your cheerful autistic hair. A second artist collapses.

Walking in the rain in new shoes is helpful. I dream December go burn why off-season. Here the roses are bathing. Open your joy, stay for a bit, I can find in your sorrow a rhythm. Tralalalalalala Tuesday.

I'm not going in to work Sunday, I depress I weep ask how I make. I love you as best I can, the world loves me, why complicate the torture and the refusal to abandon animals. I can't handle. Because yoga is red, I'm womanless and I'm just some big guy around your neck. It was winter, October returned before April on that cowboy race with a rock-music background.

Sometimes I feel Superstar like the sub at Mikes. Take the weevils out of the automobiles and glue the leaves back on the trees. I didn't feel like spending the explanation of feelings. Let's not shout in front of badly decorated shop windows.

There are ads in my picture frames just like drawings that should go to the hospital. Tonight all he wanted was Nancy in his piano and his guitar. Donovan collects seashells and dolls' hearts while crunching on ducks. You tell me about those who are frozen down to their skates. Walk in the springtime of the snails.

I can't be born any more than I've already been. Stab my ghost, I see artificial colours. My disarray involves angels with clean wings. I'd like to trade poverty. Stranger to treasures, lover of the fridge. The ship to join me has sailed, you'll never go to Venice.

I Spain the globe, depart little portable mirror. I'll put everything in the wind, even the ladder. Buy me a white dress and a shoe, so I can disguise myself in a bouffant. I hope for everything that can be excluded. Deep down I suppose I like fried blackbirds in baskets of fruit flies, carry me far from the quarrels.

Be careful, ladybugs bite when you listen to music from *The Godfather*. Come play hockey, a little snow from Beelzebub will fall on our heads. Break the ice, like I can cut out houses with scissors. I tell you nothing.

It's a crime to die at noon without breakfast and smiling among the flowers of gentle baby chicks. Chasing a spider from the house can be made into something sad, by placing it on a rock. My mayo expires February 14. Downhill skiing is pricey and swimming pool installation doesn't really interest me.

Looking out the window is no walk in the park. The world spins wrong, I'm bored squared. Her name is Isabel and his, Mario. I like shoes with a red stripe on the side.

Metal isn't my thing. *So sick,* I glue hour hands to my lungs so I can breathe new days. Sonata Arctica. Give me some time. I changed my phone number to change my voice. Maybe you'll leave in May, with Polysporin in your eyes.

A bug on my leg, removable tattoo. Gentle anemone,
sting of leaves on trees and beautiful names of life,
never bored. The poor are oblivious to the treasures
beneath the rocks. At the balloonless ball, a mirage—
your mother buried on the moon.

Which summer should the fan face to unearth the plastic zebras in the sand? Blood sugar level of cake at breakfast, it's just not sensible. Walk, walk until noon. But how are you supposed to walk in the rain? It's pissing! Giacometti's colours or Magritte's, go, comb your hair outside in the wind.

You're going too far. Short films at the Cleopatra. Too much to see, need rest but fighting energy every day not easy. I do my best, in a society of techno bio healthy as hell poutine at midnight didn't breakfast in the morning go work run. Show up late early never in between, arborescent fever.

Today, it'd take a truck to make me budge. Each evening, Francine goes bowling, her social life passes her by and she goes to bed at two in the morning despite having to work. Someone put a garden gnome on my desk and I have to find who sent it to send it to someone else.

In a kind of blur, I plunge into the amusement of Parcs Vivants. The wind carries me to vital signs and I don't talk about a movie exploring death. Go into the Avatar forest, stop dying "aren't you sick of dying, you bunch of idiots?" Claude Péloquin tells you. Psychosis in the forest of its bloody sex.

Imper*fect* me. Rid me of my obsessions in closed sounds. Nuit Blanche at the Hotel Opus, I thought I saw a piano with the legs of a horse. We stomp on ants on the bike path. We need to get the skates out of the closet, dress the fish in style, pull socks on over the shoes.

My little rainbow mist, my unwed angels fallen back into the sky. Come dance on the clouds in the lake where young paintings in flowers cry out: "look a daisy a beautiful Nathalie evening." I regret I must decline your ill-yellowed adult circumstance.

My cabbage goes to the Maxi this afternoon, a special on broccoli. Are you sure your oven's turned off before you leave? The first place you wanted to be, in the desert on a camel. My friend Jerome thought he made out his father in a car, opening the door: "Hey dad!" while realizing it wasn't his father at all.

I can't lend you a mattress for your sister, because I have only one. Every day I vomit the bus that takes me away from you. It would take me a car to get out of Sunday, drink a Lambicus Blanche there where the cats sleep in the stairwell. Watching Jacques Brel in the gold-framed mirrors.

Your beauty tells me that the mending of angels is going well. Sing me the pear before I fall in the apples. In melancholic tabulations I am YOUR wife and I love you in your dress when I'm wearing white pants. Blue October we're listening. Je souris comme une chanson étrange "Angie" car je sais la façon de ne pas marcher sur les rails quand le train va à l'ouest. I come back from the East and WD-40 has persuaded me "to live beyond my means."

You wake up next to a museum at seven in the morning without a sip of coffee. Your depression punctures the sun, it's cold outside waiting for the car heading back to Montreal. STOP. The traffic of unimportant ideas, the traffic of my ideas veers off. Buy a pack of cigarettes so you have even less money. We have poor feet in our couple of hours.

Worried, I sweat books when the mouths of whales burn with forgotten sailors like solitary snakes. Just be yourself, an invisible freedom. Snuff out your fatigue in a sunny spot. We're all going to die in the dictionary, without images to illustrate us.

The painless sky-blue alarm with strong bones and flood, the object being to break nothing. Rejection of destruction and of the unbearable joy of Rufus. Boy you're confused boy showing up at my place like I don't know you. I travel in the photos of Andrés' mind.

I fling cherries from the top of your laughter waiting for the return of Gogol's nose and drawings of seagulls on tissue boxes. Become rich to buy a new identity—like Jicheal Makson or Mijak Chelson.

To sing movement too light the dandelion fleas when I sunbathe on the lawn I forget to photograph the blue astronaut at the end of the Lachine Canal. Noon happens every day, we can be big, *Savoure le rouge mon amour*. To intervene in horizontal rain.

Choose me tomorrow to slow down the solitude of feeling the usual ascent of coming home. Just thinking of it has a cost. Everything we live matters more than the anticipation. Resounding midnight, more action than hope. Bruce Willis surfs on an airplane and Steve Irwin plays with crocodiles. Regarding Henry, nothing from nothing.

TRANSLATOR'S ACKNOWLEDGEMENTS

I'm grateful to Michelle Winters for her dedication and imagination in the first drafts of these translations. Huge thanks to Catherine Cormier for her essential contributions and valuable insights, and to Anne McLean for her excellent tips on ways to approach translation. Finally, my gratitude to Marie-Ève Comtois for trusting Michelle and me with her work, and for some spirited clarifications.

Stuart Ross

Montreal-Cobourg train, January 2015

THE AUTHOR

Marie-Ève Comtois is an administration officer at the hospital Hôtel-Dieu du CHUM in Montreal. She bikes and hikes every day and is preparing a new black-and-white magazine that explores short picture stories for those who do not have time to read. Her first book, *Le Windex de Narcisse,* was published in 2007. *My Planet of Kites* is a translation of *Je Te Trouve Belle Mon Homme*, published by Écrits des Forges in 2012.

THE TRANSLATORS

Stuart Ross is the author of about fifteen books, most recently *A Hamburger in a Gallery* (DC Books) and *Further Confessions of a Small Press Racketeer* (Anvil Press). He lives in Cobourg, Ontario.

Michelle Winters' fiction has appeared in *Taddle Creek, Dragnet,* and *This Magazine,* and has been shortlisted for the Journey Prize. Michelle works as a translator in Toronto.

OTHER BOOKS FROM MANSFIELD PRESS

Poetry

Leanne Averbach, *Fever*
Nelson Ball, *In This Thin Rain*
Nelson Ball, *Some Mornings*
Gary Barwin, *Moon Baboon Canoe*
George Bowering, *Teeth: Poems 2006–2011*
Stephen Brockwell, *Complete Surprising Fragments of Improbable Books*
Stephen Brockwell & Stuart Ross, eds., *Rogue Stimulus: The Stephen Harper Holiday Anthology for a Prorogued Parliament*
Diana Fitzgerald Bryden, *Learning Russian*
Alice Burdick, *Flutter*
Alice Burdick, *Holler*
Jason Camlot, *What The World Said*
Margaret Christakos, *wipe.under.a.love*
Pino Coluccio, *First Comes Love*
Dani Couture, *YAW*
Gary Michael Dault, *The Milk of Birds*
Frank Davey, *Poems Suitable to Current Material Conditions*
Pier Giorgio Di Cicco, *The Dark Time of Angels*
Pier Giorgio Di Cicco, *Dead Men of the Fifties*
Pier Giorgio Di Cicco, *The Honeymoon Wilderness*
Pier Giorgio Di Cicco, *Living in Paradise*
Pier Giorgio Di Cicco, *Early Works*
Pier Giorgio Di Cicco, *The Visible World*
Salvatore Difalco, *What Happens at Canals*
Christopher Doda, *Aesthetics Lesson*
Christopher Doda, *Among Ruins*
Glen Downie, *Monkey Soap*
Rishma Dunlop, *The Body of My Garden*
Rishma Dunlop, *Lover Through Departure: New and Selected Poems*
Rishma Dunlop, *Metropolis*
Rishma Dunlop & Priscila Uppal, eds., *Red Silk: An Anthology of South Asian Women Poets*
Ollivier Dyens, *The Profane Earth*
Laura Farina, *Some Talk of Being Human*
Jaime Forsythe, *Sympathy Loophole*
Carole Glasser Langille, *Late in a Slow Time*
Suzanne Hancock, *Another Name for Bridge*
Jason Heroux, *Emergency Hallelujah*
Jason Heroux, *Memoirs of an Alias*
Jason Heroux, *Natural Capital*
John B. Lee, *In the Terrible Weather of Guns*
Jeanette Lynes, *The Aging Cheerleader's Alphabet*
David W. McFadden, *Be Calm, Honey*
David W. McFadden, *Shouting Your Name Down the Well: Tankas and Haiku*
David W. McFadden, *What's the Score?*
Kathryn Mockler, *The Purpose Pitch*
Leigh Nash, *Goodbye, Ukulele*
Lillian Necakov, *The Bone Broker*
Lillian Necakov, *Hooligans*
Peter Norman, *At the Gates of the Theme Park*
Peter Norman, *Water Damage*
Natasha Nuhanovic, *Stray Dog Embassy*
Catherine Owen & Joe Rosenblatt, with Karen Moe, *Dog*
Corrado Paina, *The Alphabet of the Traveler*
Corrado Paina, *Cinematic Taxi*
Corrado Paina, *The Dowry of Education*
Corrado Paina, *Hoarse Legend*
Corrado Paina, *Souls in Plain Clothes*
Stuart Ross et al., *Our Days in Vaudeville*
Matt Santateresa. *A Beggar's Loom*
Matt Santateresa, *Icarus Redux*
Ann Shin, *The Last Thing Standing*
Jim Smith, *Back Off, Assassin! New and Selected Poems*
Robert Earl Stewart, *Campfire Radio Rhapsody*
Robert Earl Stewart, *Something Burned on the Southern Border*
Carey Toane, *The Crystal Palace*
Aaron Tucker, *Punchlines*
Priscila Uppal, *Summer Sport: Poems*
Priscila Uppal, *Winter Sport: Poems*
Steve Venright, *Floors of Enduring Beauty*
Brian Wickers, *Stations of the Lost*

Fiction

Marianne Apostolides, *The Lucky Child*
Sarah Dearing, *The Art of Sufficient Conclusions*
Denis De Klerck, ed., *Particle & Wave: A Mansfield Omnibus of Electro-Magnetic Fiction*
Paula Eisenstein, *Flip Turn*
Sara Heinonen, *Dear Leaves, I Miss You All*
Christine Miscione, *Carafola*
Marko Sijan, *Mongrel*
Tom Walmsley, *Dog Eat Rat*

Non-Fiction

George Bowering, *How I Wrote Certain of My Books*
Denis De Klerck & Corrado Paina, eds., *College Street–Little Italy: Toronto's Renaissance Strip*
Pier Giorgio Di Cicco, *Municipal Mind: Manifestos for the Creative City*
Amy Lavender Harris, *Imagining Toronto*
David W. McFadden, *Mother Died Last Summer*
Deborah Verginella, ed., *Bon Appetito Toronto!*

To order these books, please visit mansfieldpress.net